Young Learner's

Step by Step

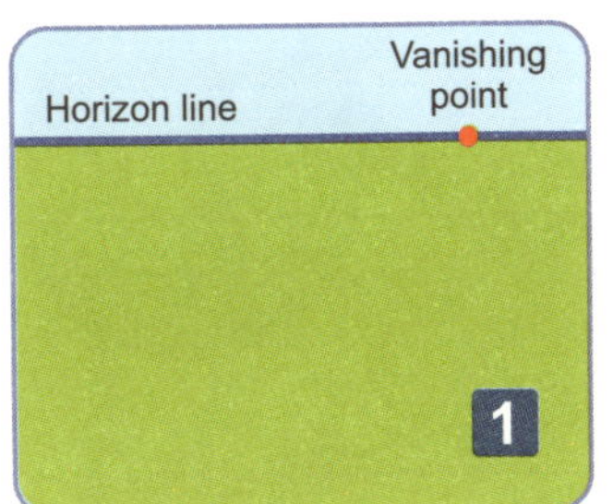

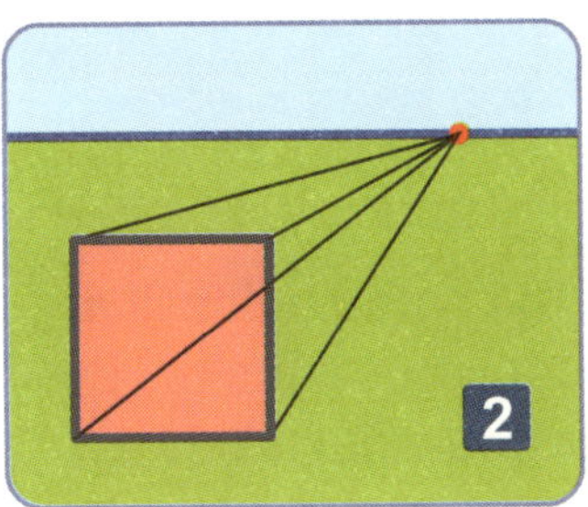

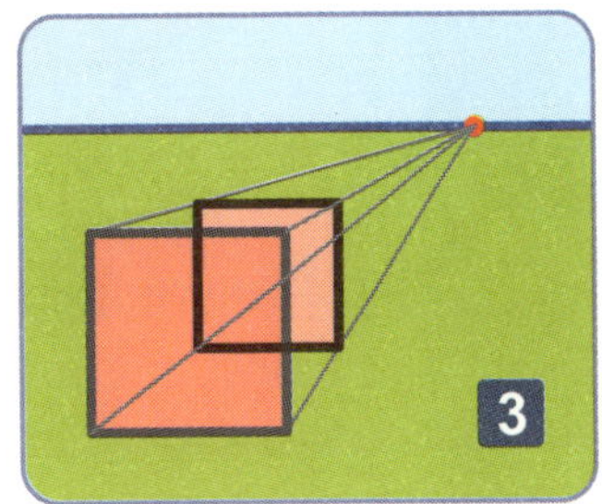

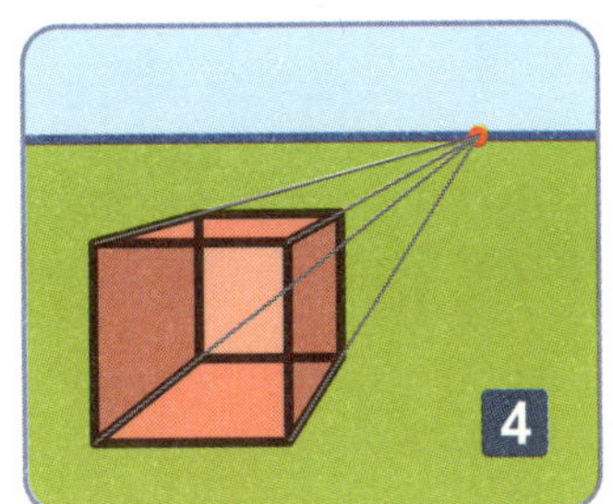

Young Learner Publications®

G-1A Rattan Jyoti, 18 Rajendra Place, New Delhi- 110 008 (INDIA)
Tel: 25750801, 25820556, 25755559 Fax: 91-11-25764396
Website: www.goodwillpublishinghouse.com
E-mail: gph.ylp@goodwillpublishinghouse.com
goodwillpub@gmail.com

One-Point Perspective

Let us first understand what exactly does the word 'perspective' mean in art. Imagine that you are standing along a straight open road on a grassy plain—the road, trees, fences and power poles—are all diminishing towards a single spot far ahead of you. This is a simple example of a perspective and is called one-point perspective. Thus, perspective drawing is a drawing technique used to illustrate dimensions on a flat surface.

Carefully observe and read all the steps to understand the one-point perspective.

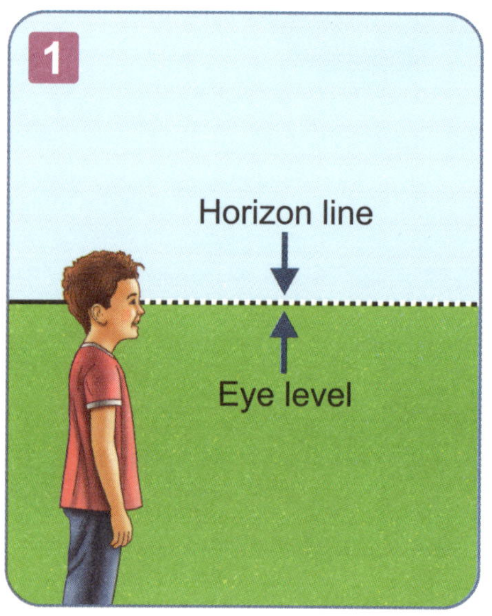

We make a simple one-point perspective cube using the three main elements of perspectives: 1. **Horizon line**
2. **Vanishing point**
3. **Lines**

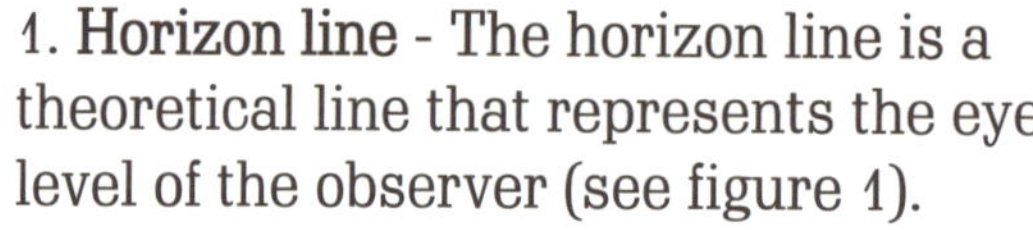

1. **Horizon line** - The horizon line is a theoretical line that represents the eye level of the observer (see figure 1).

2. **Vanishing point** - It is the point (usually) on the horizon line where receding lines (planes) converge (see figure 2).

3. **Lines** - To make a cube, all diagonal lines must intersect at a point on the horizon. All vertical lines are perpendicular to the horizon or will form a 90° angle when intersecting the horizon. All horizontal lines are parallel to the horizon. They never intersect with the horizon (see figure 3).

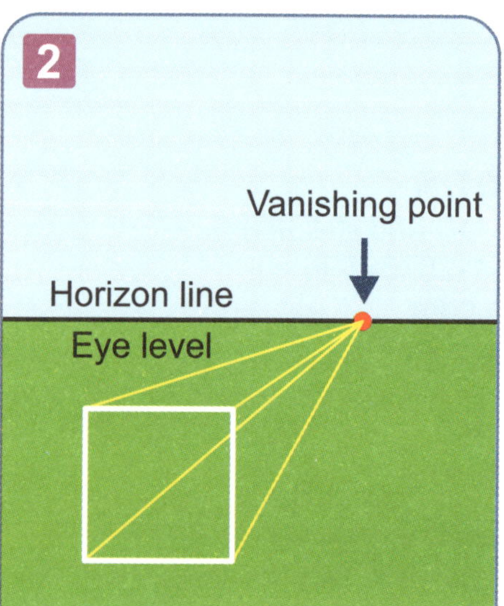

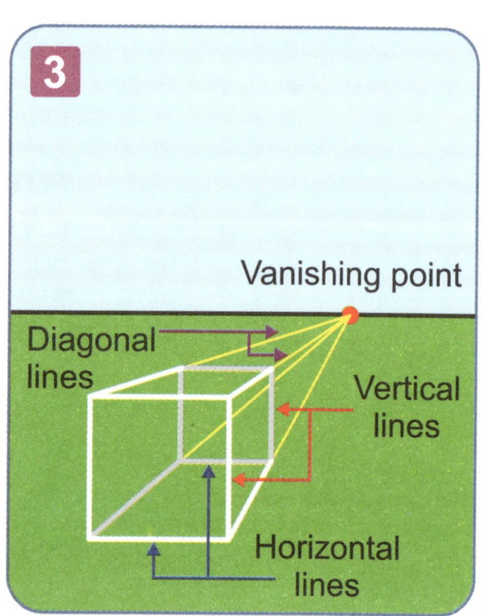

In this lesson, we shall learn to draw a cube in one-point perspective, below the horizon line. It will provide a solid foundation for all our drawings.

1. Draw a horizon line. Then draw a vanishing point.
2. Now, draw a square (face of the cube). Next, using a light pencil, draw diagonal lines from four corners of the square to meet at the vanishing point.
3. Once again, draw a small square parallel to the first square within the diagonal lines.
4. Join the four corners of both the squares with a dark pencil.

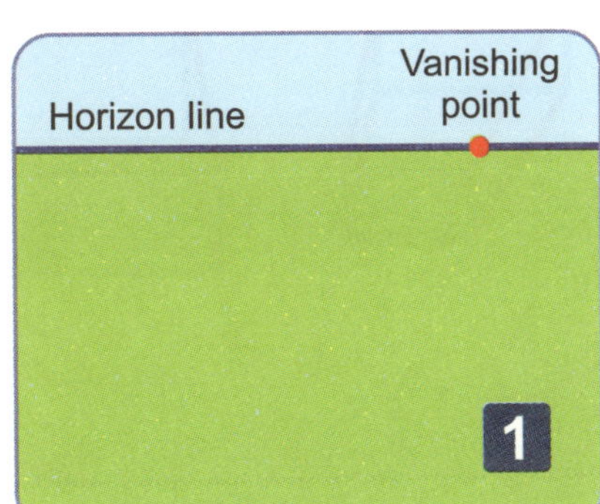

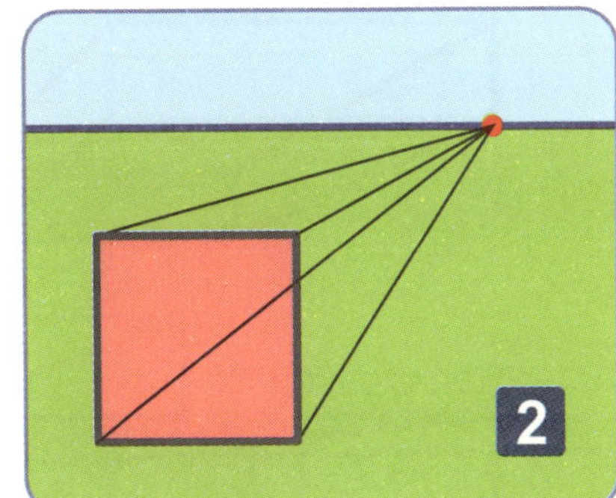

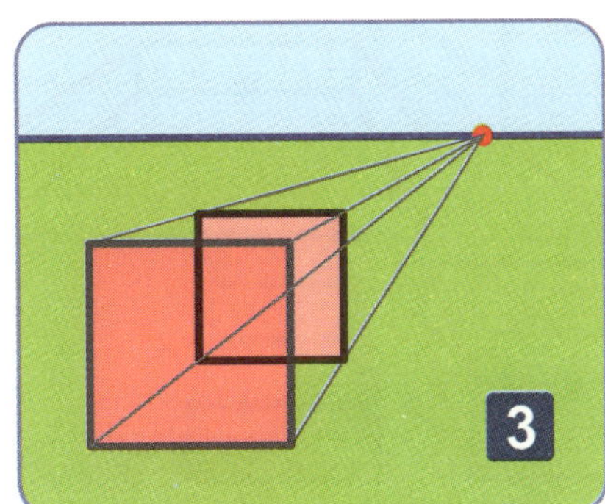

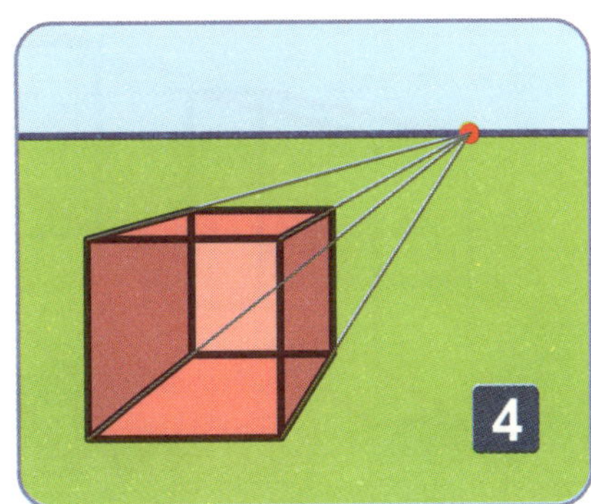

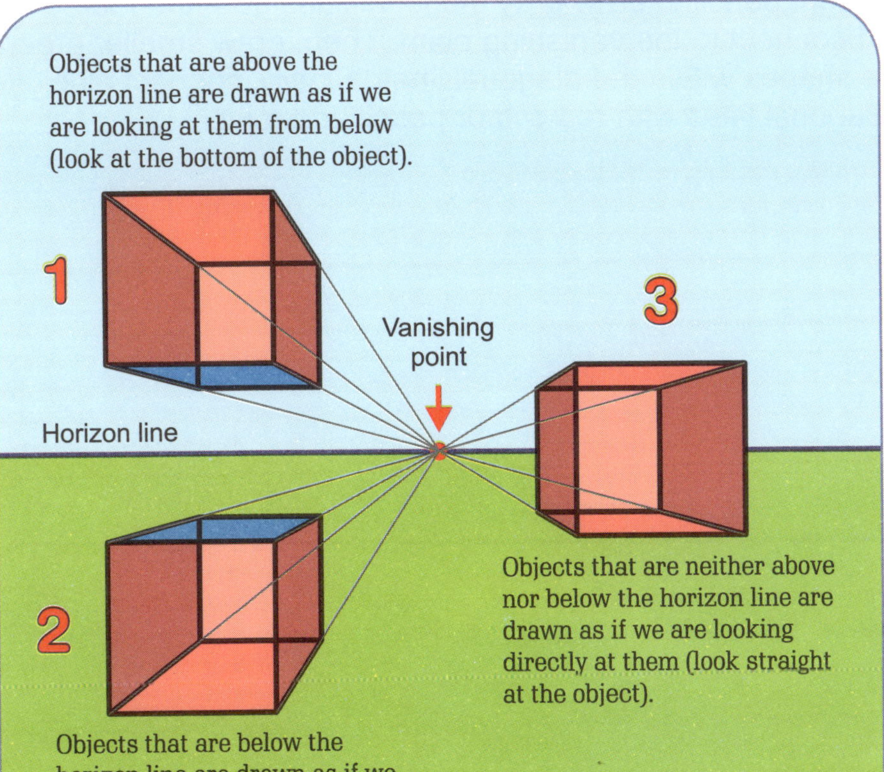

Look at the figure carefully and learn to draw a cube in one-point perspective below and in line with the horizon line.

In this exercise we will practise drawing different shapes above, at the centre and below the horizon line in one-point perspective.

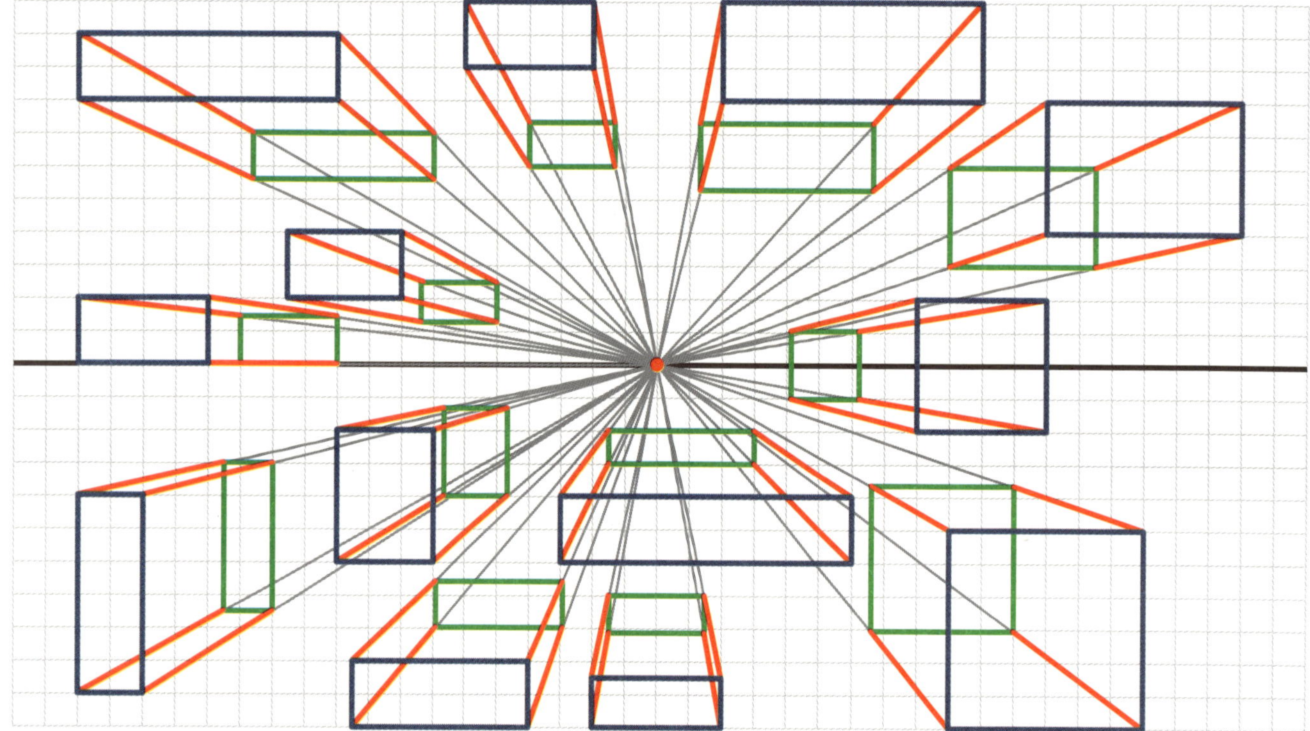

Observe the above figure carefully and copy it in the graph below. First draw the blue squares and rectangles. Use a light pencil to draw grey diagonal lines from the four corners of the blue shapes and connect to the vanishing point. Then, draw smaller green shapes parallel to the first blue shapes within the diagonal lines. Finally, connect blue and green shapes along the diagonal lines with red colour pencil and ruler.

In this exercise, we shall practise drawing a room, based on one-point perspective. Please note that the grey lines indicate the completed steps.

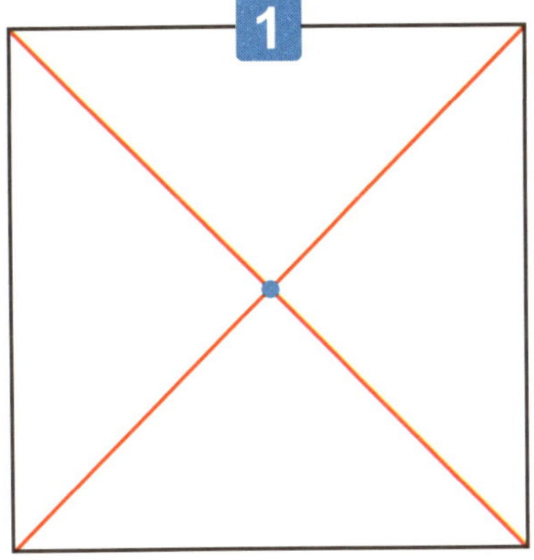

Use a light pencil to draw an 'X' at the centre of the square paper. This gives you the vanishing point.

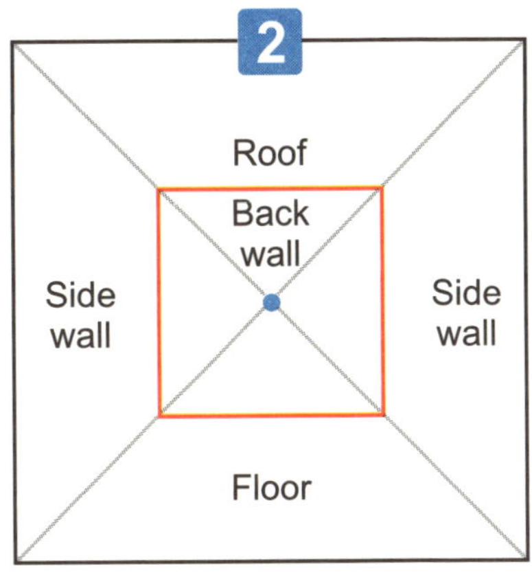

Draw a square to make the back wall, side walls, roof and floor of the room.

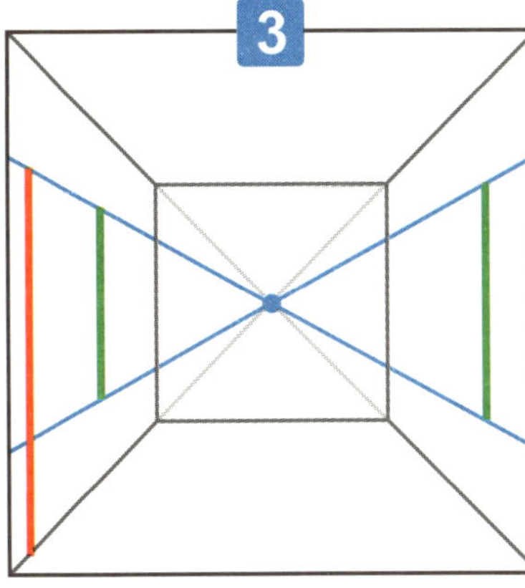

Use a light pencil to draw four blue lines that meet at the vanishing point. Then draw vertical lines—red for door and green for windows.

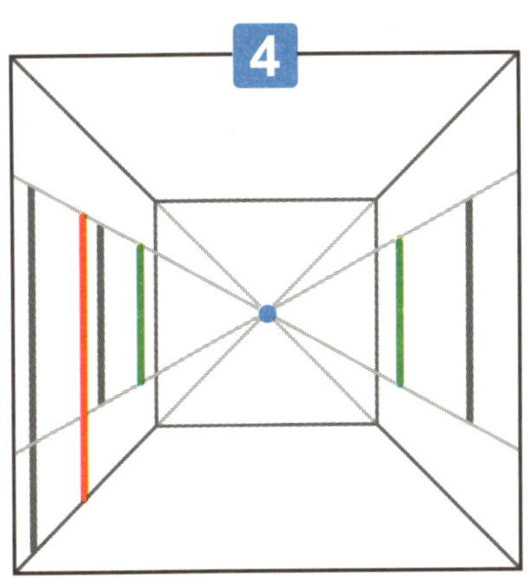

Add more vertical lines—one red for door and two green for windows.

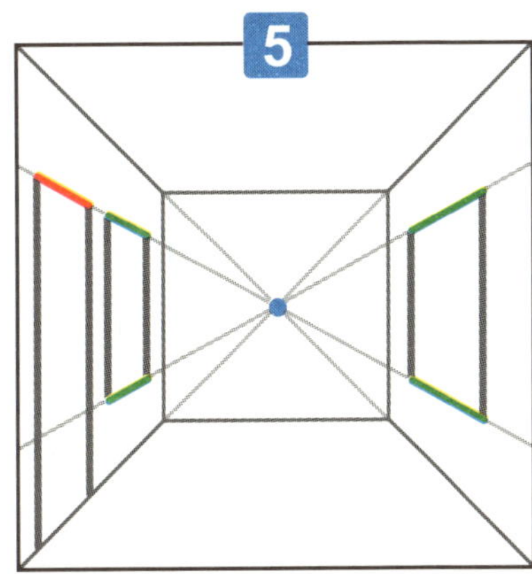

Draw a red line for the top of the door and four green lines for the top and bottom of the windows.

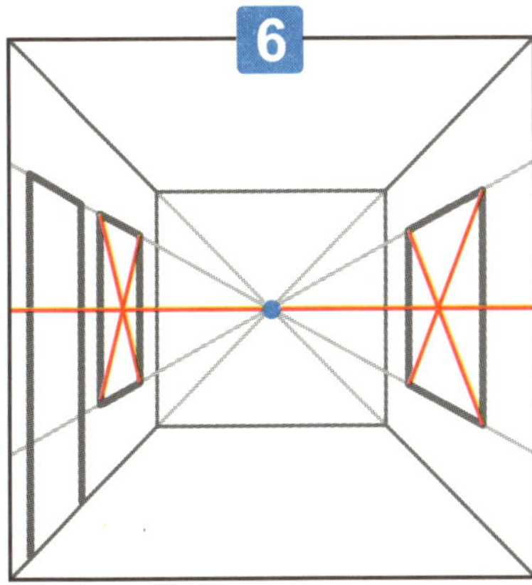

Use a light pencil to draw a horizontal line and two 'X' at the centre of the windows.

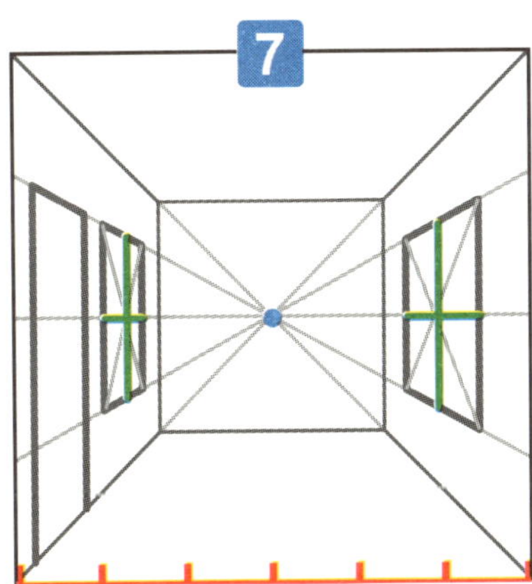

Draw green horizontal and vertical lines passing through the centre of the 'X' of the windows. Then, divide the floor into six equal parts.

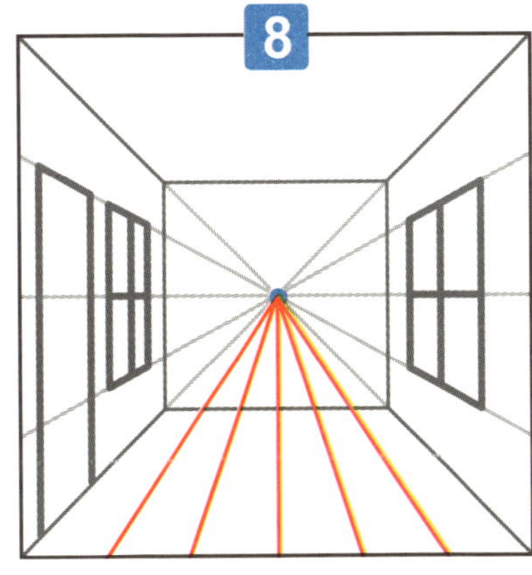

Use a light pencil to draw five lines from the vanishing point to the markings on the floor.

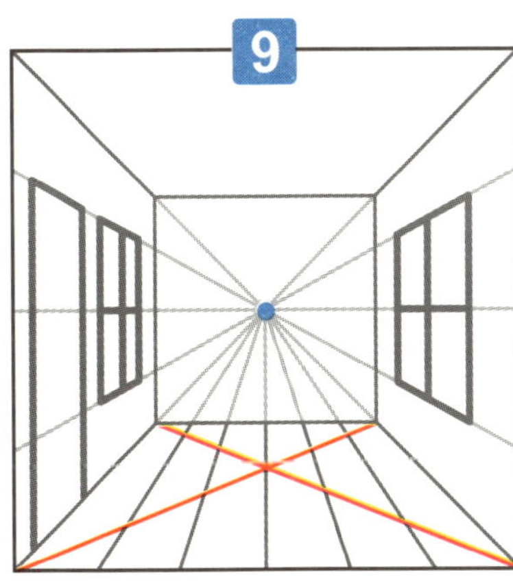

Use a light pencil to draw an 'X' on the floor.

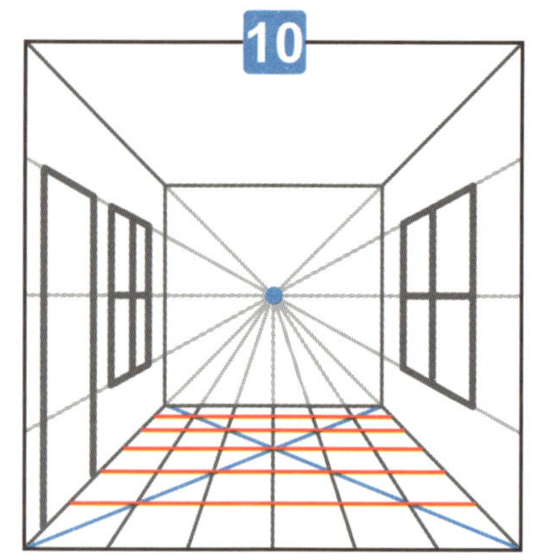

Draw red horizontal floor lines through the meeting points of floor lines and 'X'.

Erase all reference lines. The room is now complete.

Colour the drawing with colour pencils.

Follow the steps from 1 to 12 and draw a room in the box given below.

Carefully read the steps to draw the table and the chair with the help of a cube by using one-point perspective.

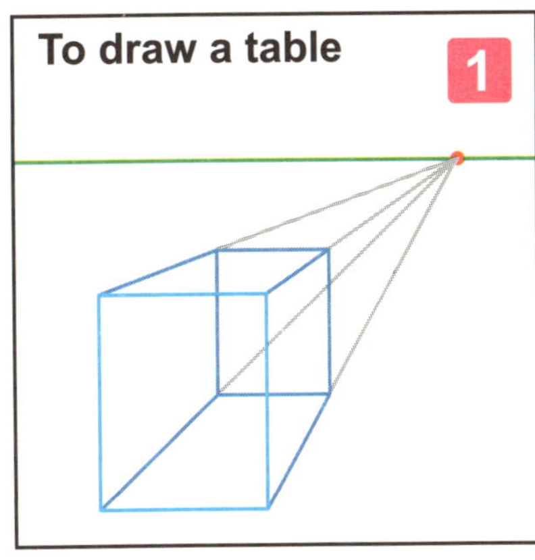

For drawing the table, draw a rectangular box shape with the help of a horizon line, vanishing point and diagonal lines.

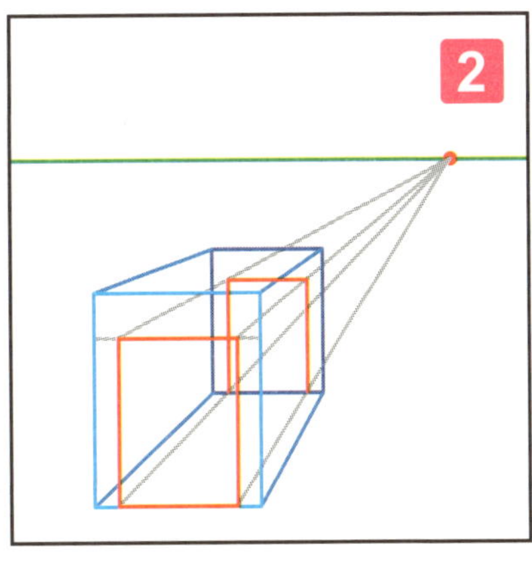

Draw two rectangles in the front and back of the rectangular box.

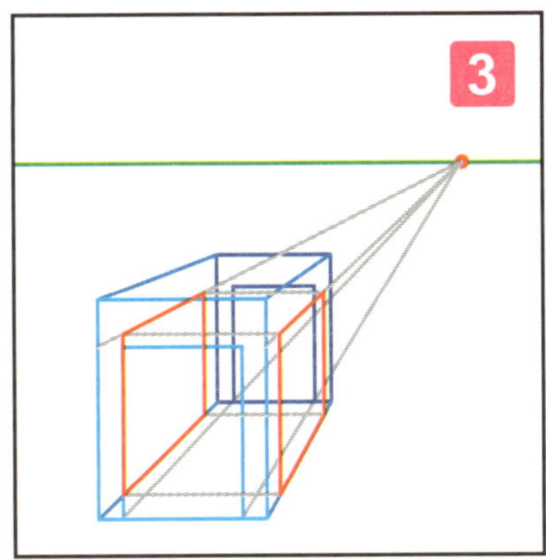

Draw two rectangles on the left and right side of the rectangular box.

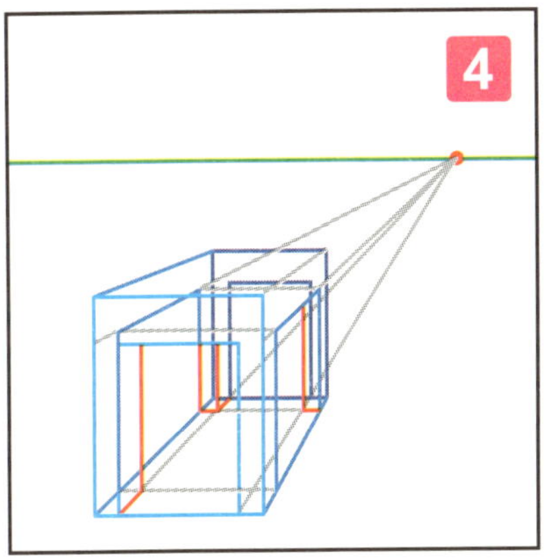

Now, draw dark vertical and diagonal lines to make the legs of the table (shown in red).

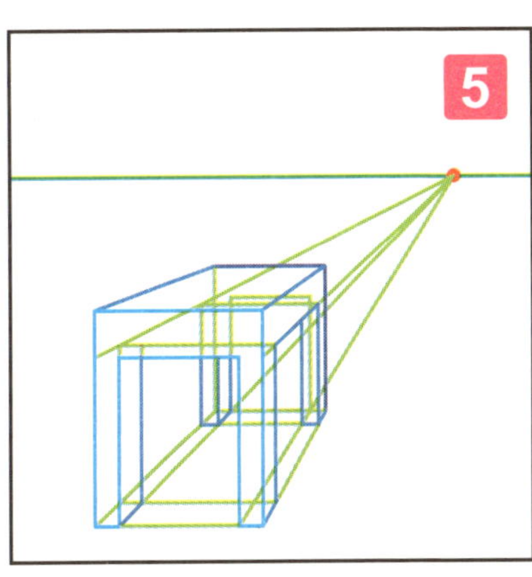

Erase the lines shown in green.

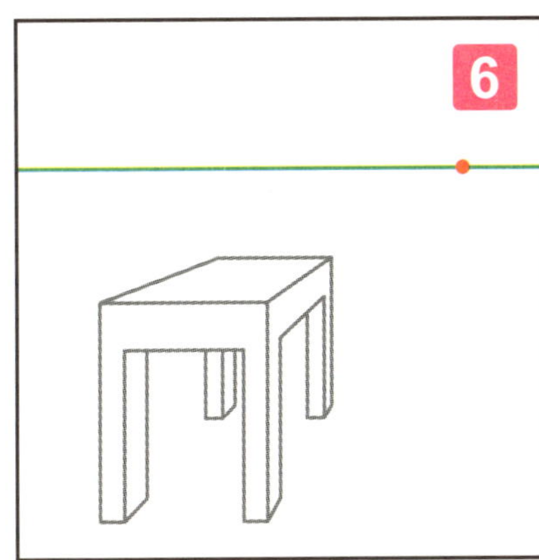

Now, your table drawing is complete. Darken the final lines using a dark lead pencil.

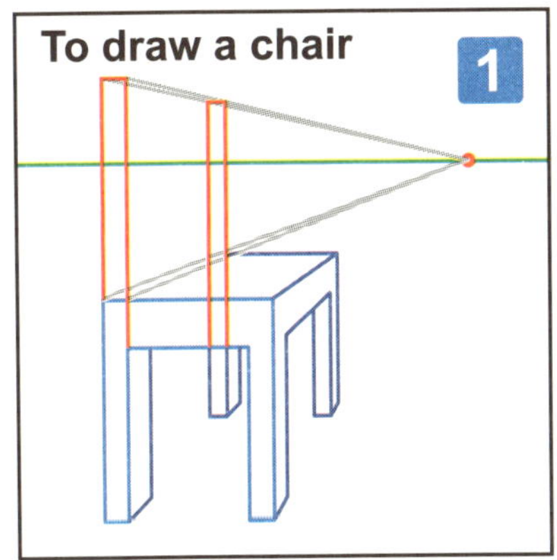

For drawing the chair first draw a table and then extend the front and the back leg lines (on the left side) above the horizon line.

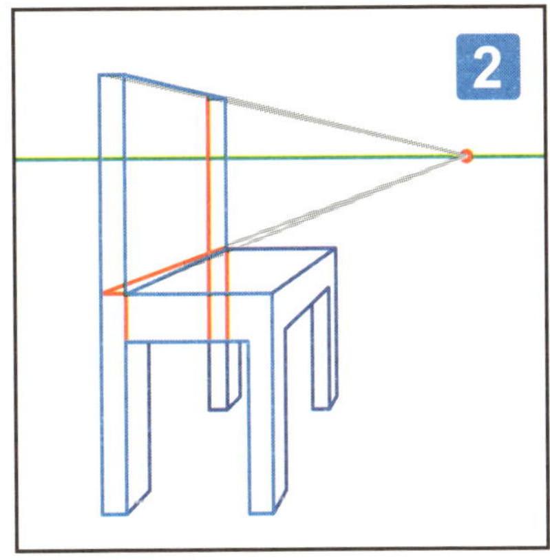

Now, erase the red lines and the diagonal lines. Darken the blue lines with a pencil.

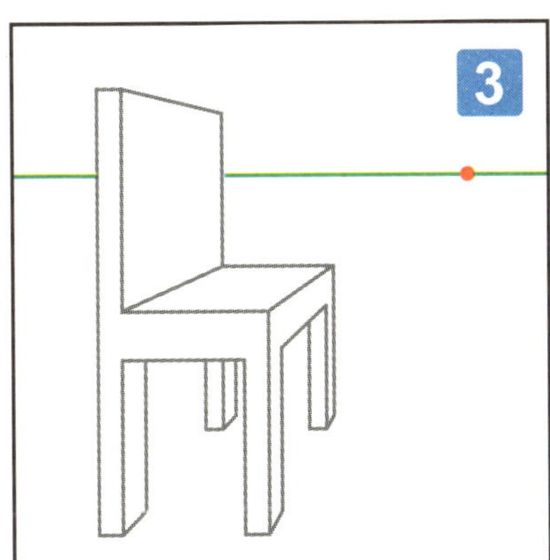

Your chair drawing is ready.

Follow all the steps given on the previous page. Draw the table and the chair with the help of a lead pencil and a ruler in the boxes given alongside. First step has been done for you.

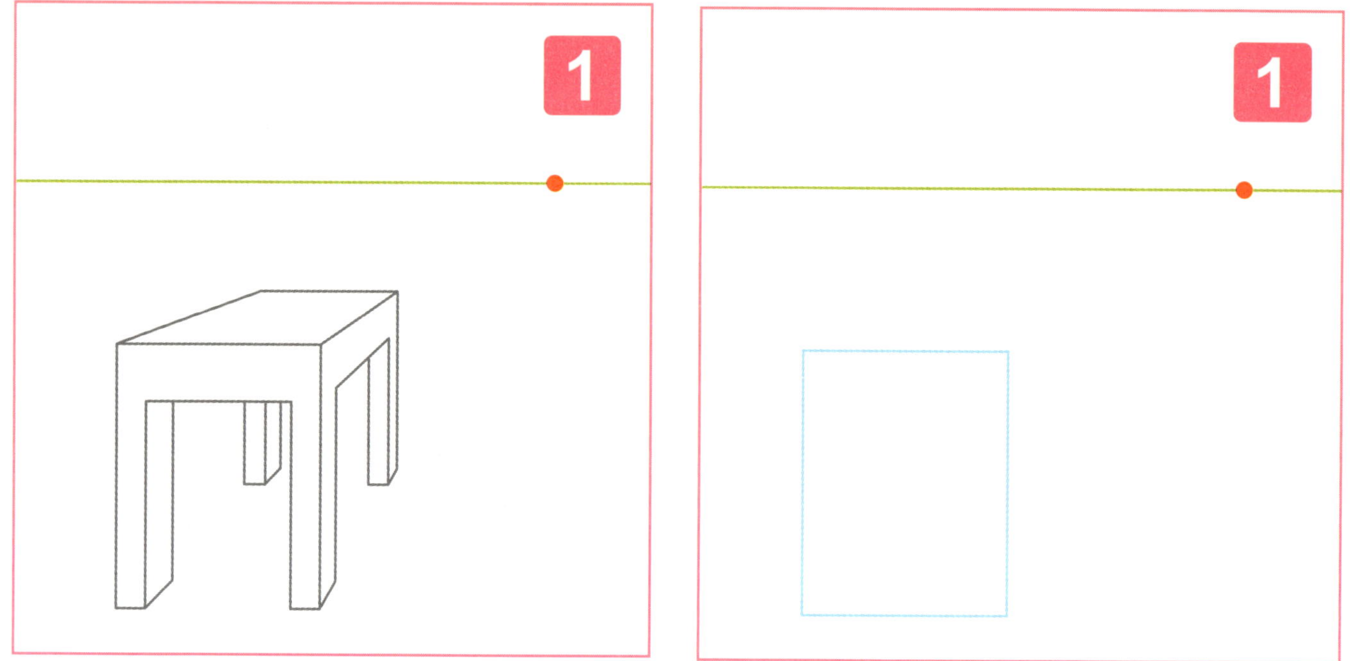

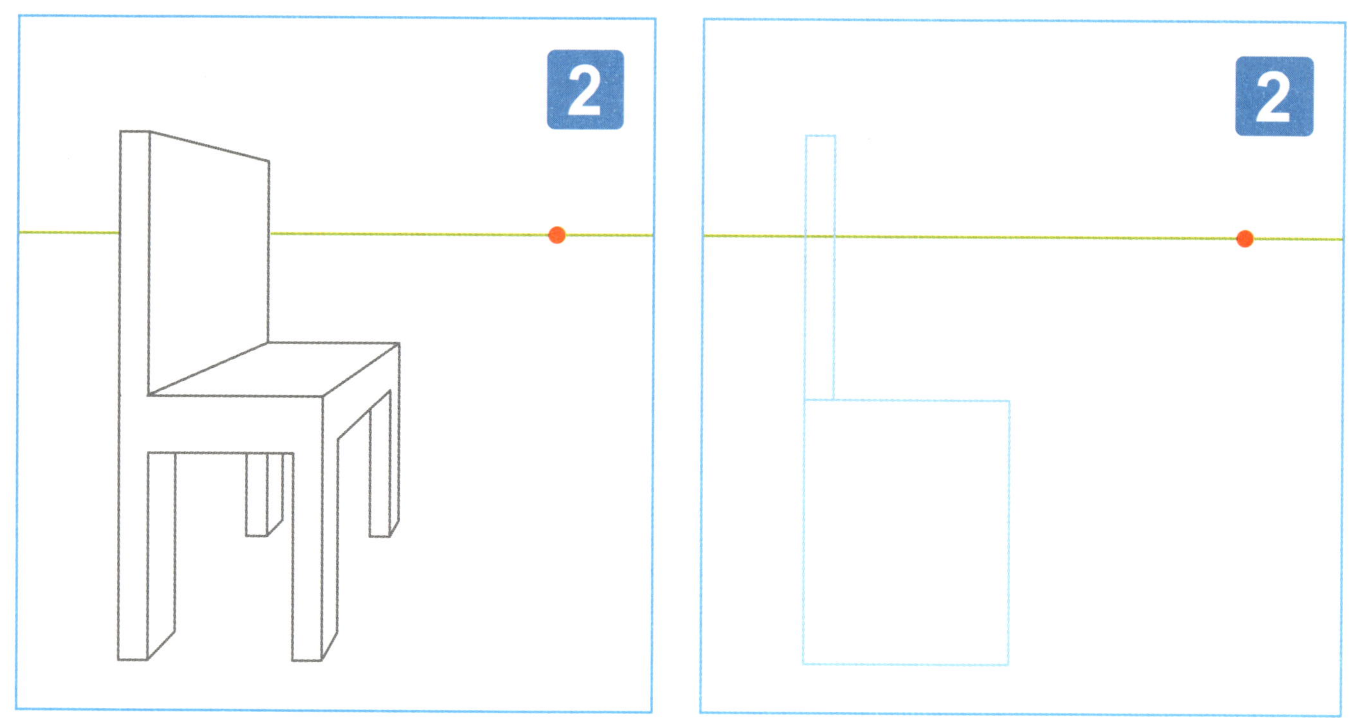

For teachers and parents: Besides this exercise, encourage the children to practise drawing other objects like book, shoe box, bed, sofa, etc. They should also be encouraged to draw the objects from different angles using one-point perspective technique.

Street Scene

In this exercise
we will practise drawing a simple
street scene based on one-point perspective.
We have studied box, table, chair and room in the
previous pages. If we look at the street drawing
given below and imagine we are placing
boxes of different sizes on a long road,
the entire exercise would seem
very simple.

Observe the street scene carefully. You will notice that all the white diagonal lines of buildings, side windows and the road meet at the vanishing point. Also, the front window sizes are linked with side windows' diagonal lines.

Study the three scenes given below. We have drawn the same two buildings from three different views by just changing the horizon line and vanishing point.

Ideal view for street scene

Ideal view for city scene

Ideal view for showing the selected buildings

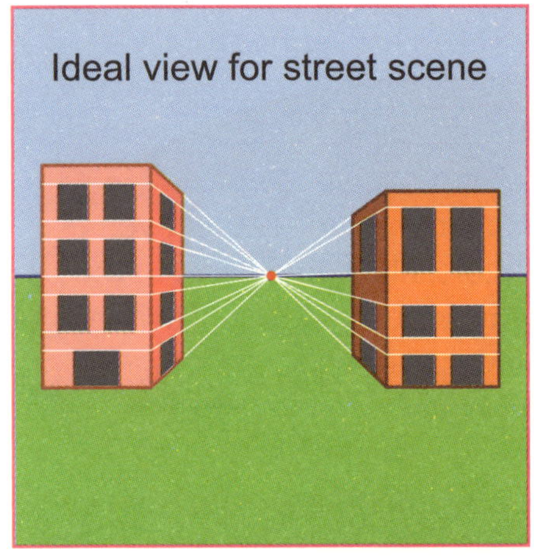

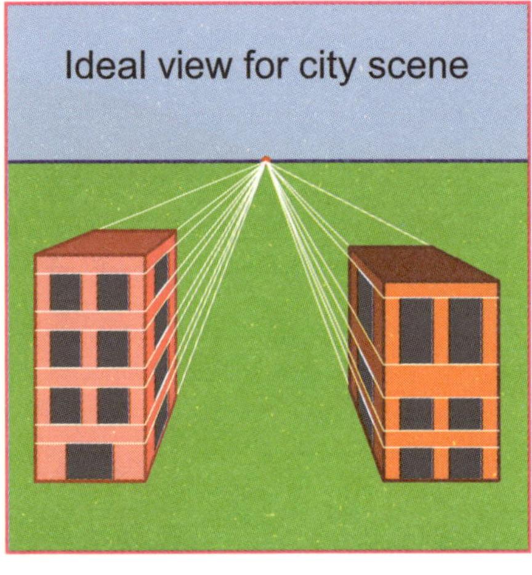

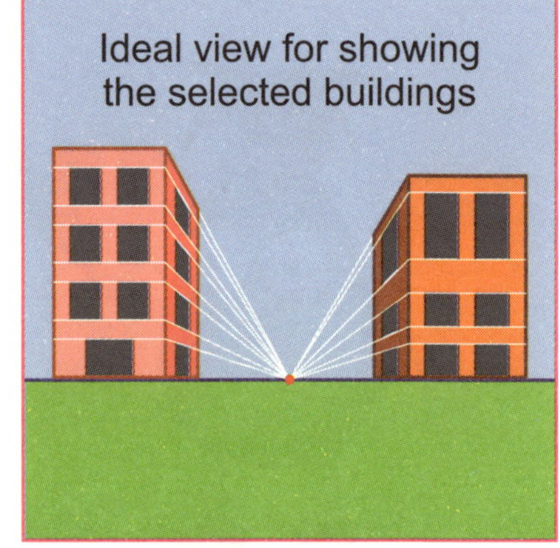

Draw a street scene with the help of a lead pencil and ruler in the box given below. Colour the drawing with crayons. The horizon line, vanishing point and diagonal lines have been already drawn for you.

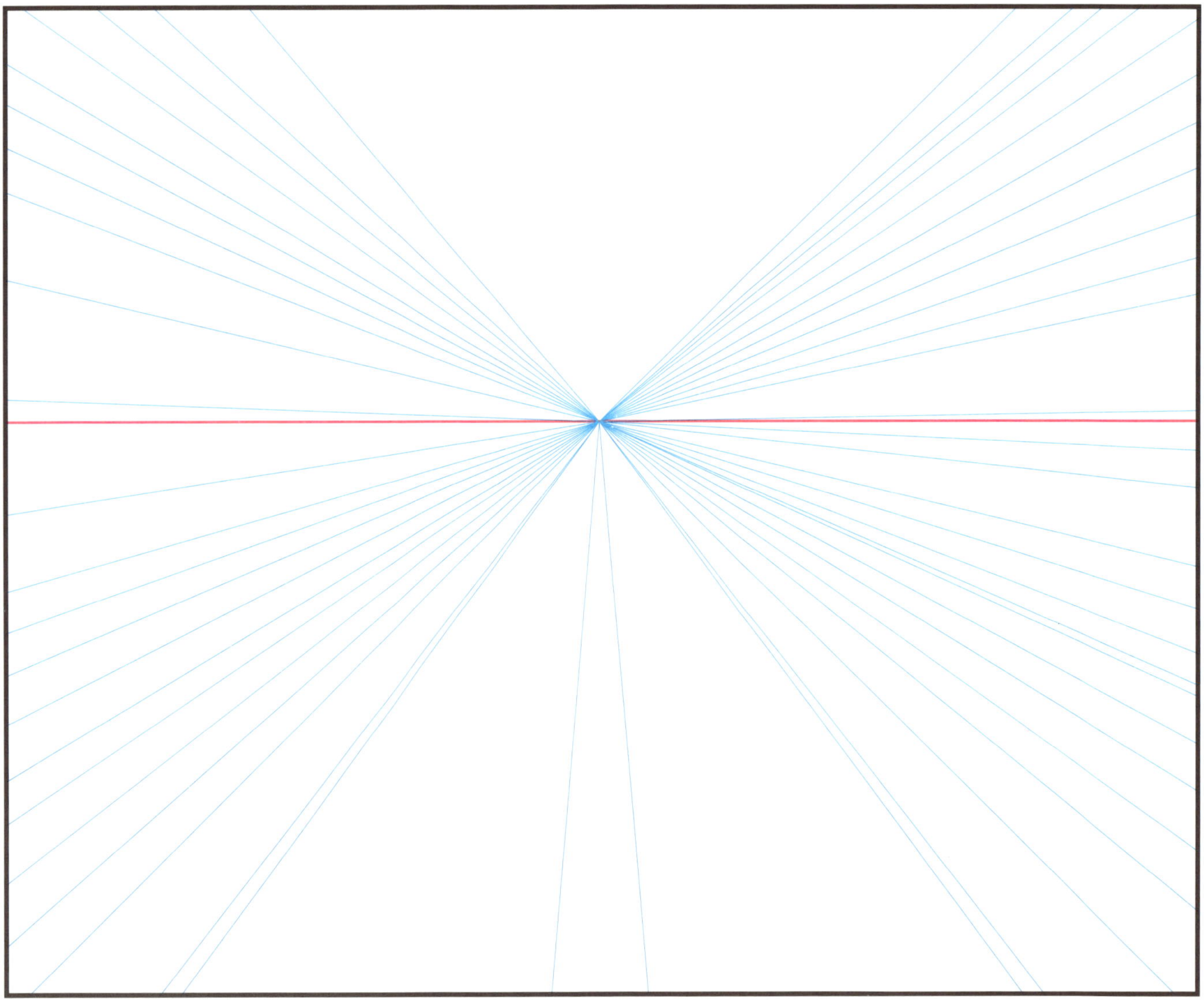

Two-Point Perspective

In two-point perspective two vanishing points are used. The horizontal line will not be used. In this case, all vertical lines are perpendicular to the horizon line. All diagonal lines intersect at both points on the horizon line, and opposite diagonal lines intersect with one another. Now, we shall learn to draw objects using a two-point perspective.

Carefully read all the steps to understand how to draw using the two-point perspective.

Horizon line

Vanishing point 1

Vanishing point 1

Centre line

1

Draw a green horizon line. Now, mark two vanishing points (with red colour), one each on left and right side of the horizon line (as shown above). Draw a dotted centre line.

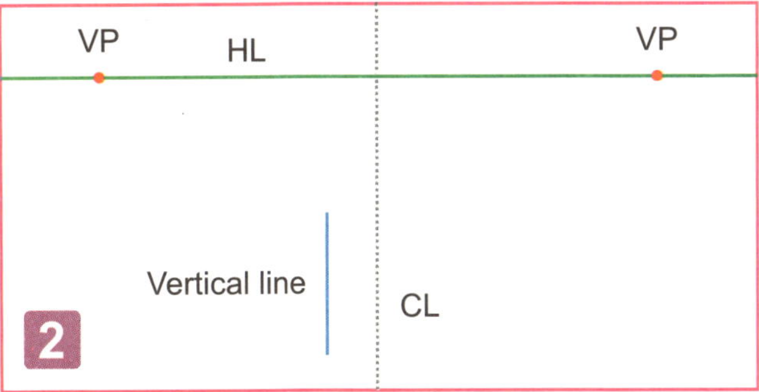

For making a box, draw a blue vertical line. Remember that if we draw the blue vertical line on centre line (shown in dotted line) we will see left and right side of the box equally. But if we draw the blue vertical line on the left side of the centre line (as shown above) we will see the right side of the box more clearly than the left side of the box (see figure 5).

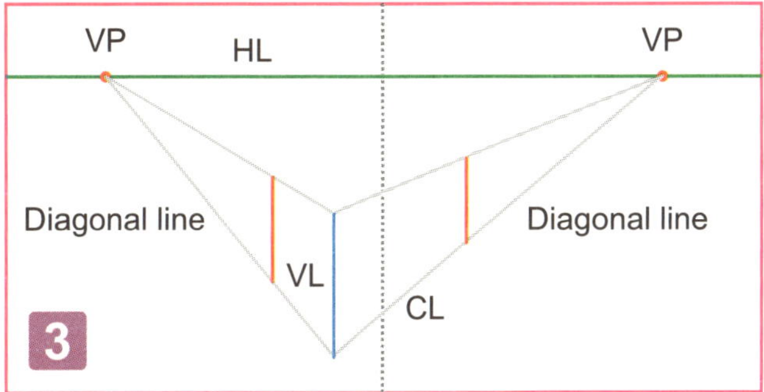

Draw lines (in grey colour) from the top and bottom of the blue vertical line to the two vanishing points. Then, draw two vertical lines (in red colour) on either side of the blue vertical line (as shown above). Remember that the size of the box depends on these two red lines.

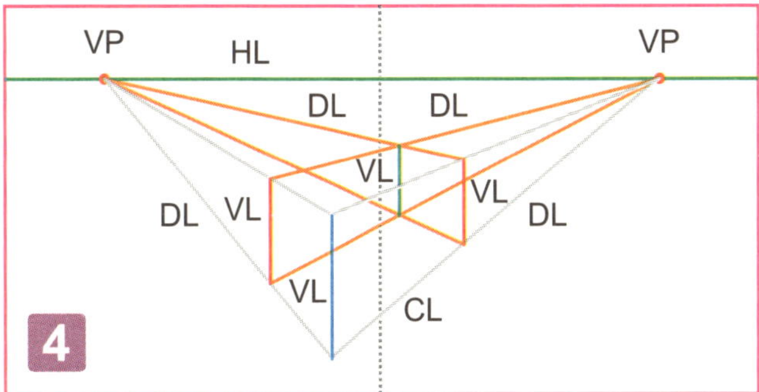

Draw two diagonal lines (in orange colour) from the top and bottom of each red vertical line to the vanishing points. Now, draw the fourth vertical line (in green colour) as shown above.

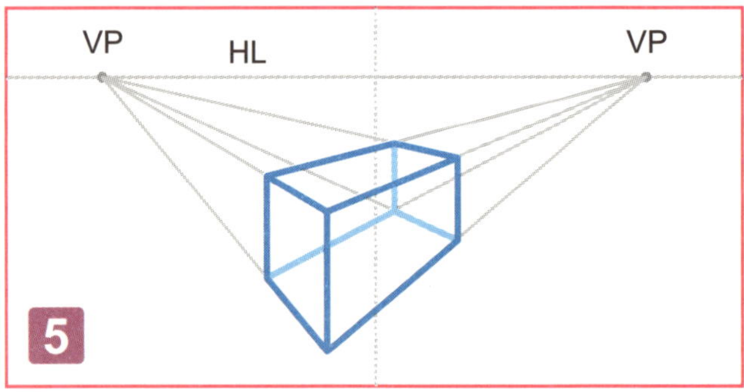

Darken the front box lines with dark blue colour pencil. Then, draw the back box lines with light blue colour. Erase all the diagonal lines and marks that lie outside the box.

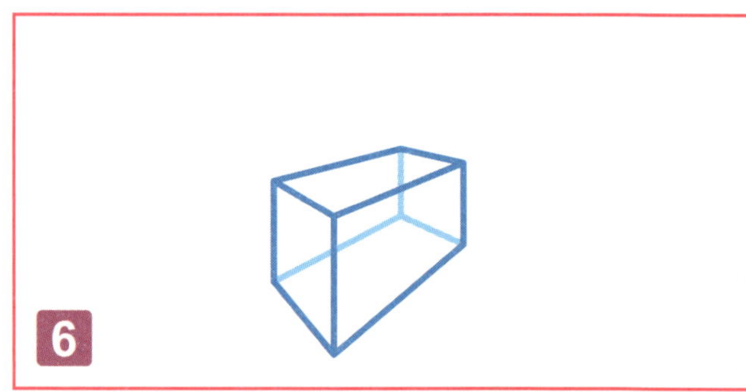

Our box drawing is now complete. Besides this box, you can also experiment drawing different angles of the box by just changing the position of the first vertical line and vanishing points.

In this exercise we shall practise drawing the three angles of the boxes in two-point perspective. Observe the given figure carefully and draw the same in the blank space given below. The first step has already been done for you.

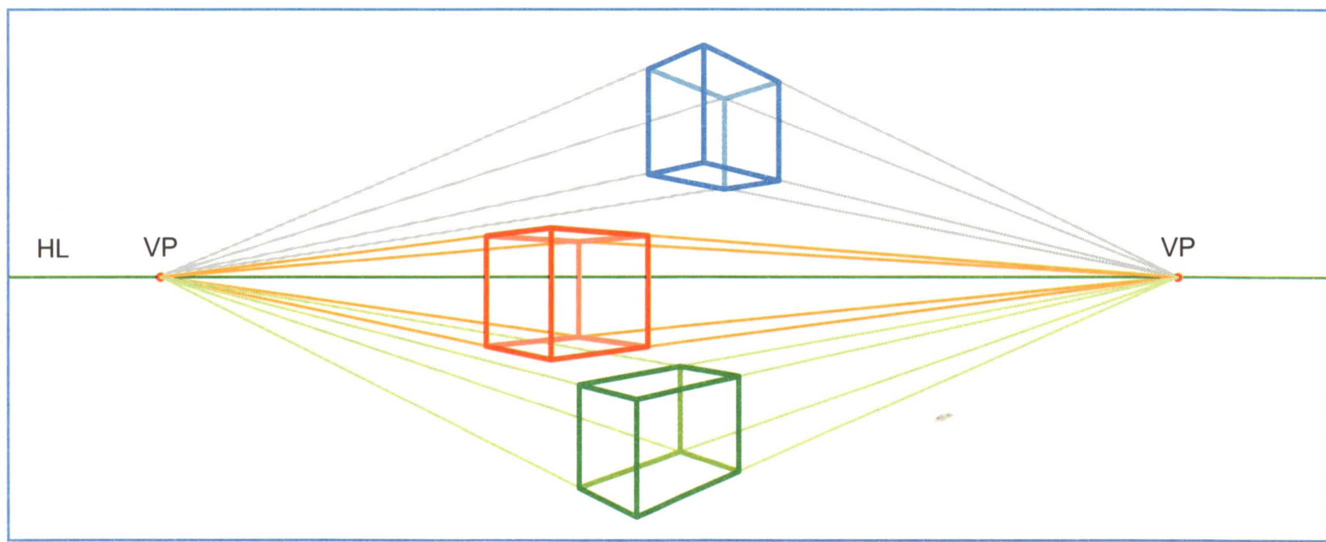

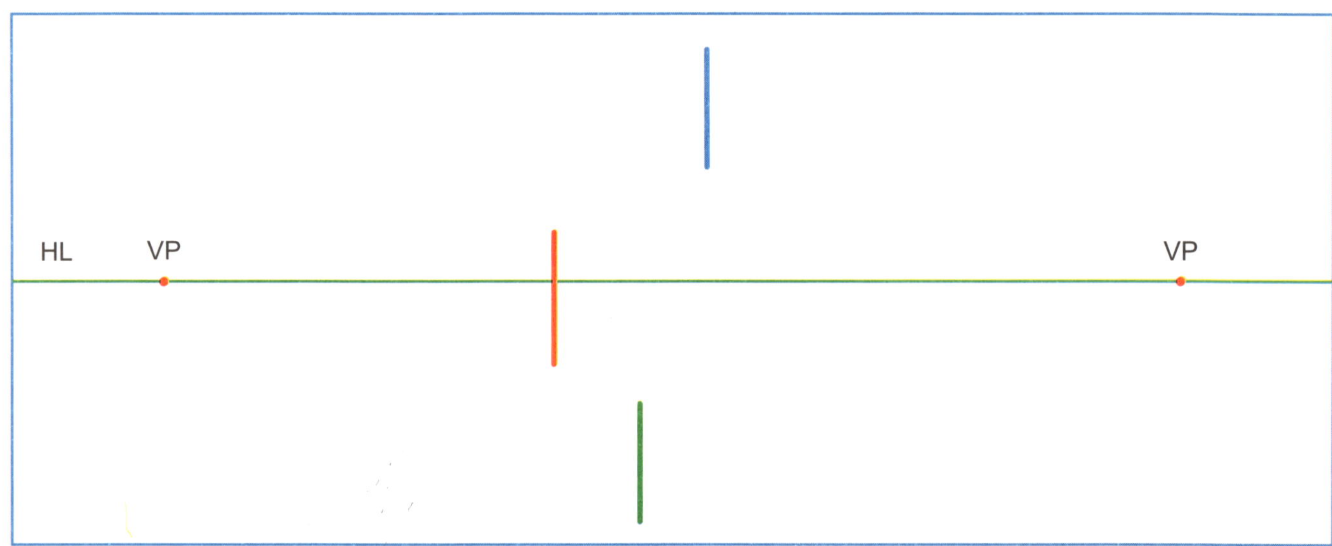

In two-point perspective two vanishing points are used when the corner of the object is facing the viewer. As shown below, if you stand in front of a street corner you can see that the left and right side of the road and buildings look smaller towards the vanishing points. Observe the street scene carefully. Copy using a lead pencil and ruler. Colour the final drawing with crayons. First step has been done for you.

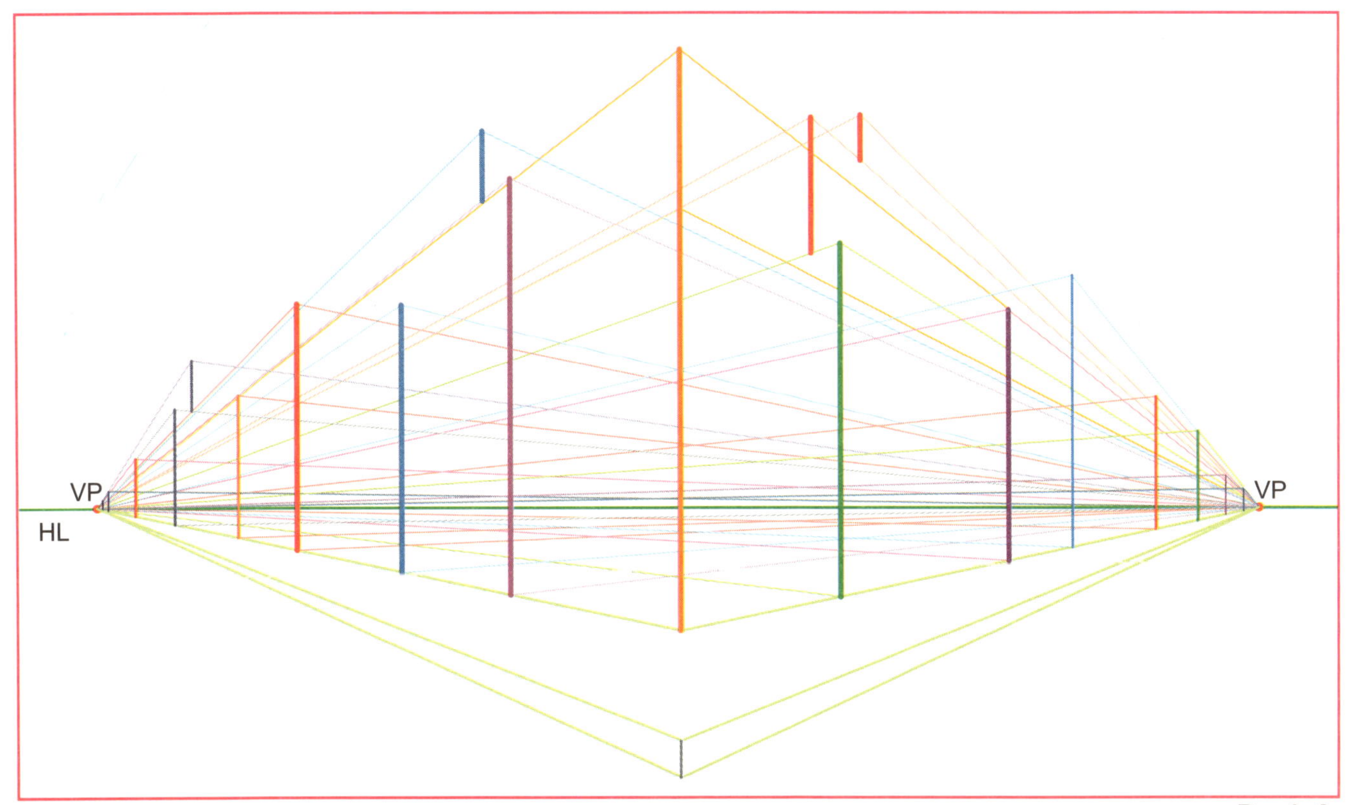

Three-Point Perspective

In the previous exercises we learned to draw using one and two-point perspectives. In three-point perspective there are three vanishing points. Two vanishing points are located along the horizon and the third vanishing point is located either above the horizon or below the horizon. Imagine you are looking up at a very tall building or perhaps looking down from a great height. These extreme vantage points would best be depicted using the three-point perspective.

Carefully read all the steps of drawing a building with up and down views in three-point perspective.

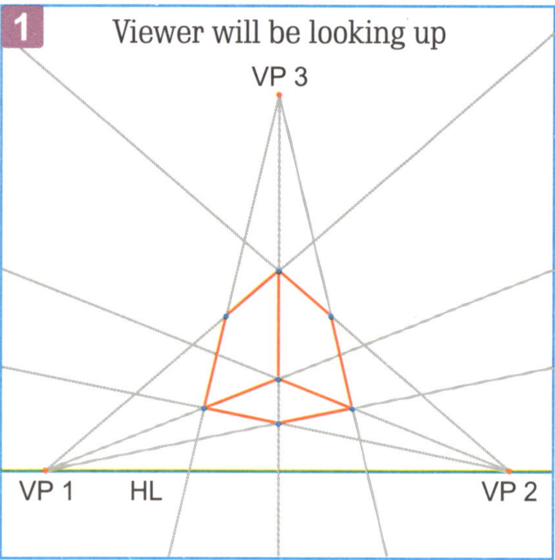

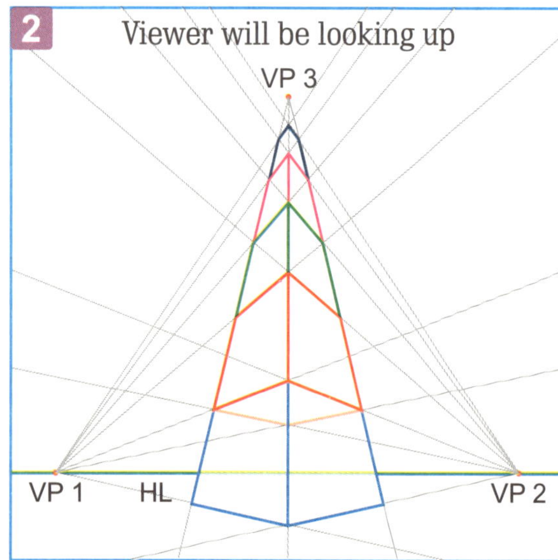

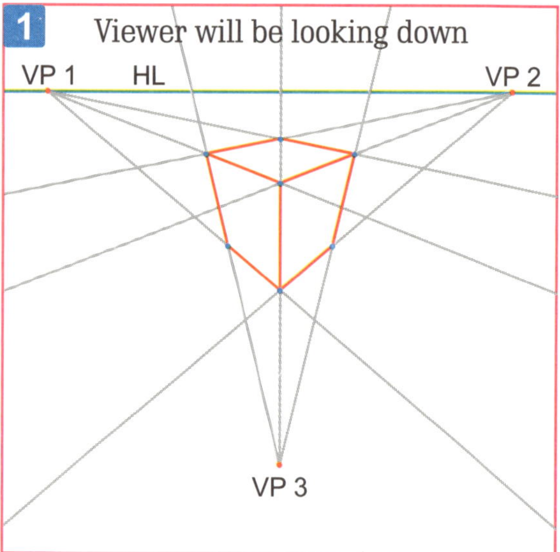

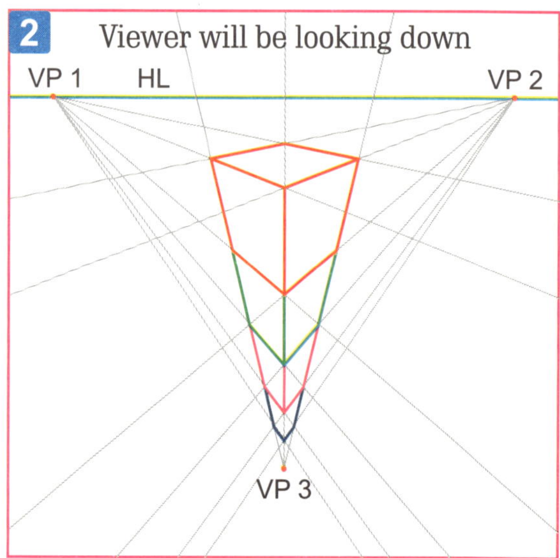

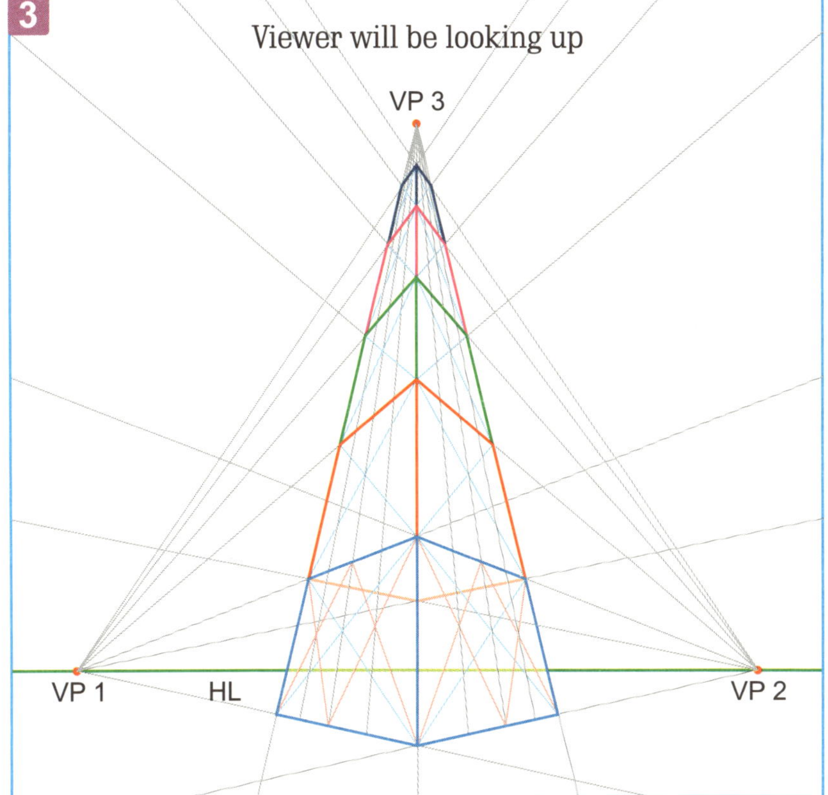

Three-point perspective is the least used form of linear perspective. This is ironic since three-point perspective is closely related to how we actually see things. The right way to consider this viewpoint would be to imagine looking up at a very tall building. All vertical construction lines lead to the third vanishing point.

If you place your third vanishing point above the horizon line, you create an image from the *'Worm's Eye View'* (looking up).

If you place your third vanishing point below the horizon line, all vertical construction lines lead to the third vanishing point. You thus create an image from the *'Bird's Eye View'* (looking down).

If you are looking down from a high-rise building you will see roofs and sides of smaller buildings. This is ideal to draw a city scene with buildings, roads, trees etc. from the bird's eye view. This can also be used for drawing city map and directions.

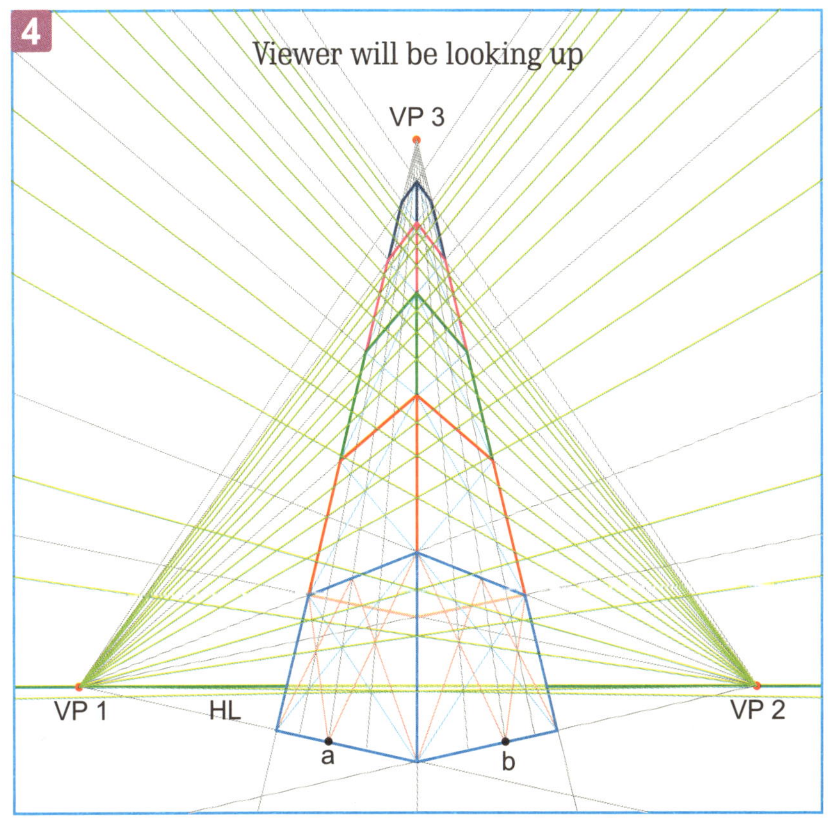

For making windows on various floors of the building, draw 'X' in light blue colour on both sides of the floor. Draw a diagonal line from vanishing point 3 and passing through the centre of 'X' and touching the bottom blue lines at points a and b. Next, draw two 'X' in pink colour on the left and the right side of the diagonal line. Now, draw two diagonal lines from the vanishing point 3 to the centre of the two pink 'X'. Draw green diagonal lines from the vanishing point 1 and vanishing point 2 to the centre of the three 'X' and draw the windows for all the floors. Remember, all the green lines will touch on the point where the light blue (X-shaped) lines cross the grey lines (see figures 3, 4 and 5).

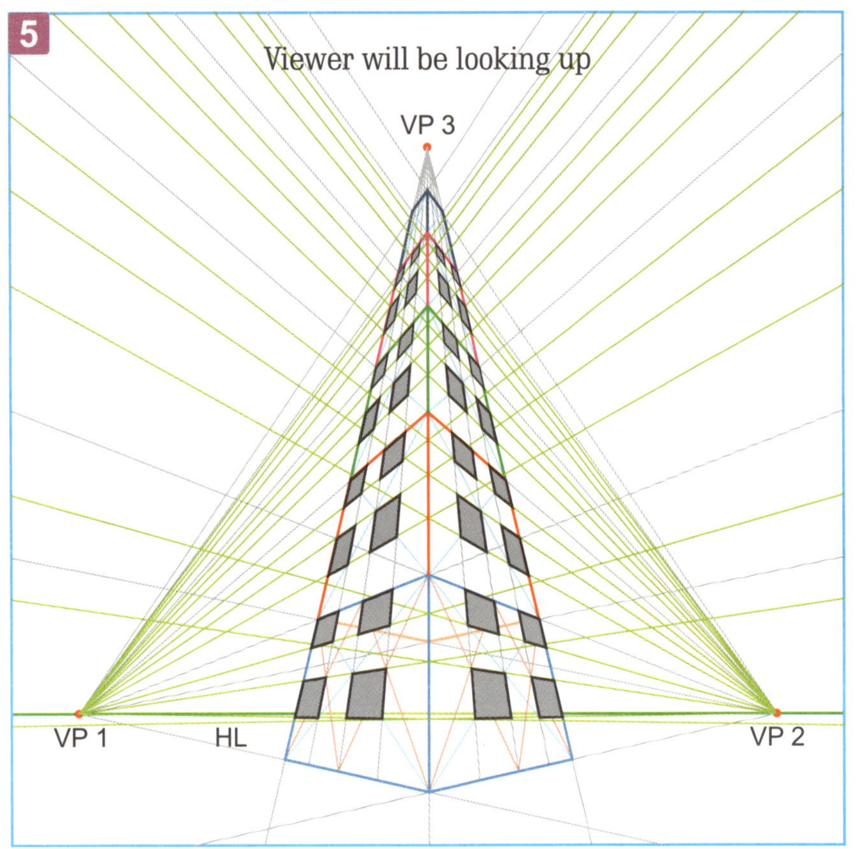

Draw the left side windows along the green diagonal lines that come from vanishing point 1 and grey lines that come from vanishing point 3. Next, draw the right side windows along the green diagonal lines that come from vanishing point 2 and grey lines that come from vanishing point 3 (as shown in figure 5).

This is a very simple way to make a complex building with windows. This technique is also used to draw a cluster of buildings. You can also change the position and number of the windows as per your requirement by increasing the number of green diagonal lines coming from vanishing points 1, 2 and 3.

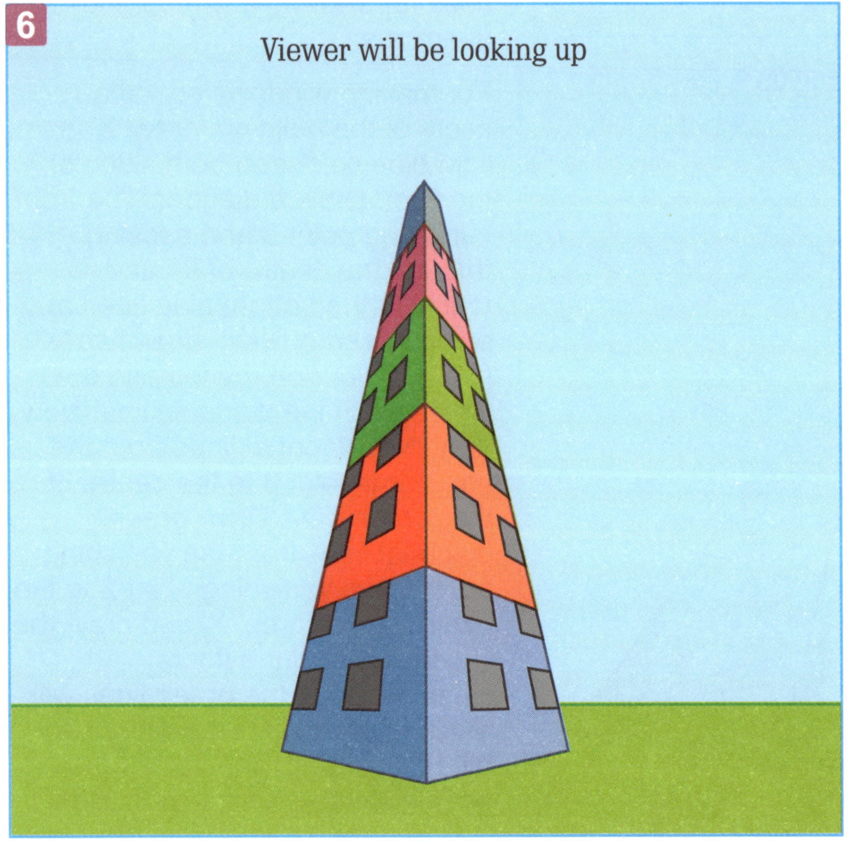

Erase the diagonal lines and darken the final outlines of the building and windows (as shown in figure 6).

For further practise draw the building in your sketchbook by carefully following all the steps. Remember to draw all the diagonal lines with a very light colour so that after completing the drawing they can be erased neatly. Once you have drawn the building, use crayons or colour pencils to colour it.

For teachers and parents: Besides this exercise, encourage the children to practise drawing different types of buildings in their sketchbooks.